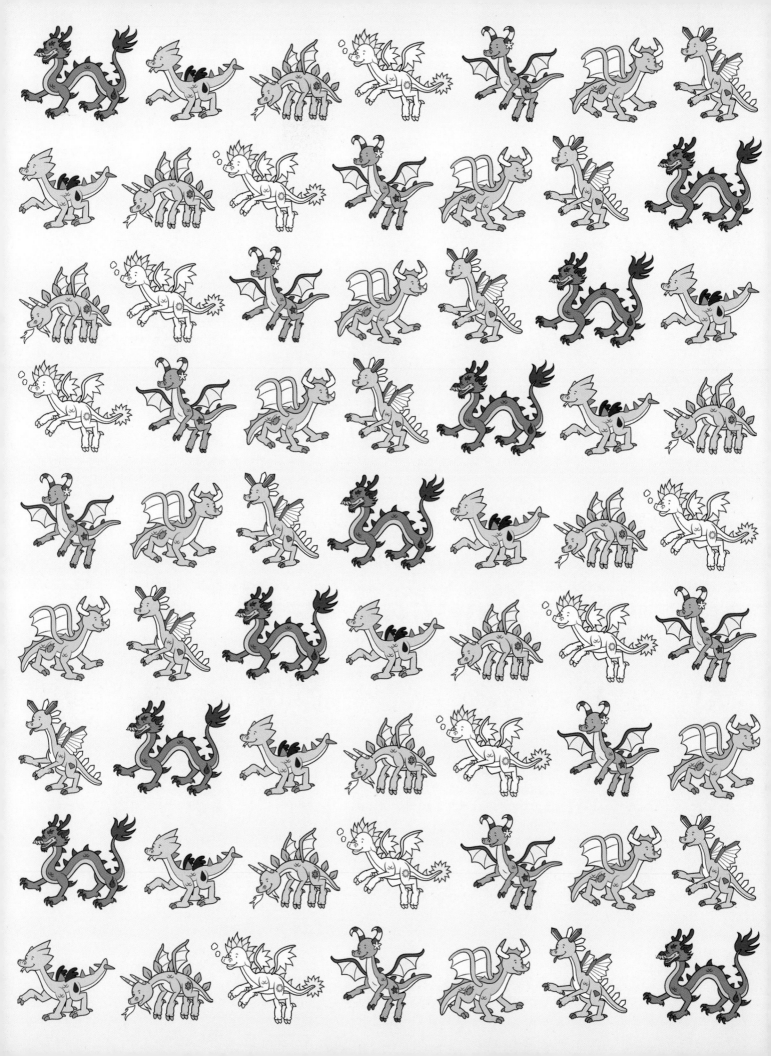

WHERE'S THE DRAGON?

ILLUSTRATED BY PAUL MORAN, ADRIENN GRETA SCHÖNBERG,
JORGE SANTILLAN, GERGELY FÓRIZS, JOHN BATTEN AND ADAM LINLEY

WRITTEN BY IMOGEN CURRELL-WILLIAMS AND FRANCES EVANS

DESIGNED BY TALL TREE, ZOE BRADLEY, JOHN BIGWOOD AND JADE MOORE

Michael O'Mara Books Limited

INTRODUCTION

Blaze, the wise elder-dragon of Thunder Valley, and his flight of dragon apprentices are preparing for a very important adventure. For the first time in centuries, they are saying goodbye to their home and travelling into new realms. The dragons can't wait to explore these enchanted and exciting destinations – from a midnight forest and a masquerade ball to a fairground and a tulip garden.

Can you find Blaze and his six fire-breathing students in every scene? They are doing their best to blend in, so you'll have to search high and low. All the answers are at the back of the book, where you'll also discover spotter's checklists for additional things to find. Get set for a scaly search adventure!

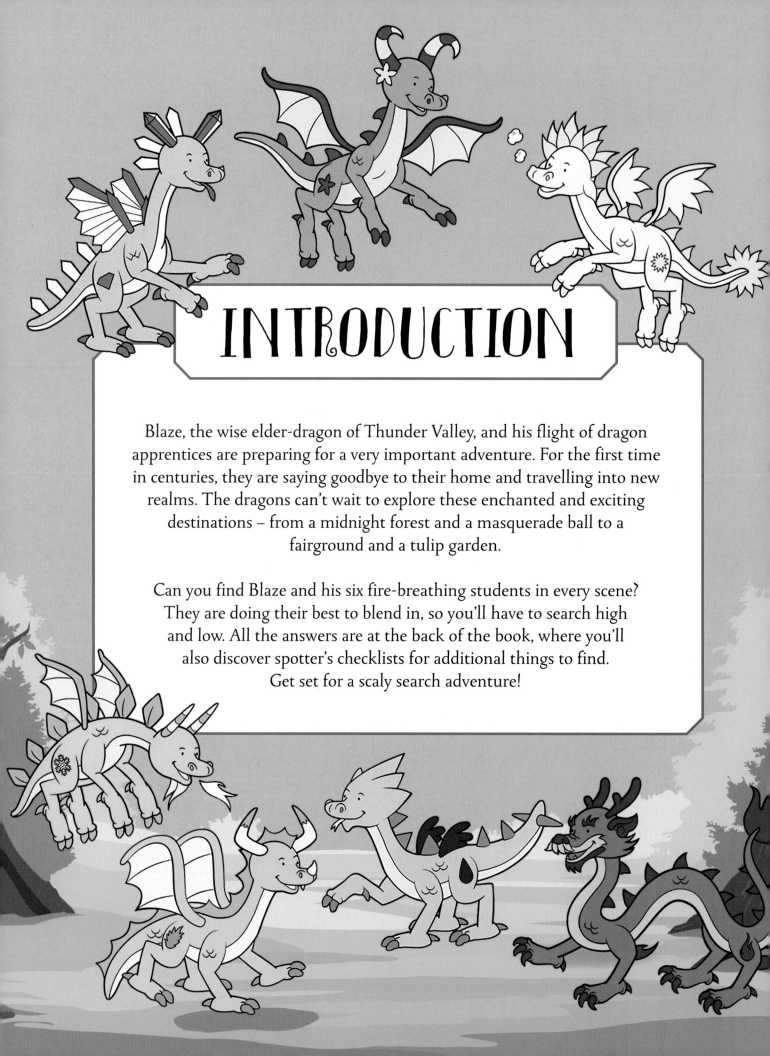

THE DRAGONS

QUINN

Magical power: Can time travel

Best known for: Extravagant horn accessories

Favourite food: Strawberry sorbet

Can't wait to: Explore new realms

BLAZE

Magical power: Can see into the future

Best known for: His wise words

Favourite food: Vegan hot dogs

Can't wait to: Make new friends

VIOLET

Magical power: Turns rocks into gemstones

Best known for: Telling jokes

Favourite food: Crystallized bugs

Can't wait to: Visit the magical Crystal Caves

STELLA

Magical power: Produces heat from her tail

Best known for: Her radiant smile

Favourite food: Star-shaped cookies

Can't wait to: Meet other flying beasts

DRACO

Magical power: Can speak all 254 dragon languages fluently

Best known for: The horn on the end of his nose

Favourite food: Jellied eels

Can't wait to: Visit the fairground

MOONBEAM

Magical power: Can conjure and control the elements

Best known for: Her appetite

Favourite food: Dragonfly skewers

Can't wait to: Discover new food

FROST

Magical power: Turns things into ice

Best known for: Being the coolest member of the group

Favourite food: Ice cream

Can't wait to: Freeze things

DRAGON CASTLE

The dragons are saying goodbye to their friends at the castle of Thunder Mountain before they set off on their trip. They haven't left the realm of Thunder once in the last 200 years, so they're excited to get going – even if their long-distance flying is a little rusty.

Moonbeam's bidding farewell to the phoenixes and has promised to send them a postcard. Meanwhile, Stella's just flown through the enchanted waterfall – its waters are said to give dragons luck before a journey.

Can you spot all of the dragons?

DAY OF THE DEAD

The dragons have arrived in Mexico, just as the famous Day of the Dead celebrations are getting underway. People are spilling into the streets wearing colourful costumes and masks. The dragons can't resist joining the fun.

Moonbeam wants to try some sugar skulls and has headed into the crowd to find a food stall. Blaze has gate-crashed the parade and is trying to persuade a dancer to help him with his face paint.

Can you spot all of the dragons?

MAGICAL MAZE

This gigantic labyrinth is a crossing point between human and enchanted worlds, and it's filled with magical beings on their travels.

The dragons aren't sure which route to take. Draco was in charge of the map, but he sneezed and it's been burnt to a crisp! Fortunately, Quinn's taken charge and is getting advice from a snufflefoot – a hairy, purple beast, renowned for its sense of direction.

Can you spot all of the dragons?

BALLOON FESTIVAL

The dragons love flying, so they're intrigued to visit this hot-air balloon festival. People have come from miles around to watch hundreds of colourful balloons take off into the sky.

Violet has decided to rest her wings and hitch a ride with some humans. She keeps trying to ignite the balloon herself, which her new-found friends find a bit unsettling. Stella and Draco are going to keep their claws on the ground to watch the display.

Can you spot all of the dragons?

ROCKY WILDERNESS

The dragons have landed in a strange stony landscape, home to a huge herd of magical horses as well as some mysterious rock dragons.

While Frost has a race with the flying horses, Draco is plucking up the courage to speak to a rock dragon. They spend most of their time asleep in caves, only venturing out into the open once every 50 years to sunbathe, so it's quite an honour to be able to talk to them.

Can you spot all of the dragons?

FAIRGROUND FUN

The dragons have never been to a fairground before – they're very excited and can't wait to have a go on these rides.

Draco is trying to squeeze himself into a dodgem car and Stella's having fun chasing the horses on the carousel. Blaze has settled right in and put himself in charge of the coconut shy. Moonbeam, meanwhile, is searching for a toffee apple to get her fangs stuck into.

Can you spot all of the dragons?

FLIGHT SCHOOL

The dragons have been invited to spend the day at a renowned flight school and share their super flying skills with its magical students.

Moonbeam is showing the baby flying horses how to take off, while Violet is demonstrating the best way to do a perfect loop-the-loop. Quinn's taken the opportunity to brush up on her fire-breathing technique. She is getting tips from a champion dragon who has won the 'Fiercest Fire-Breather Award' three years running.

Can you spot all of the dragons?

TULIP GARDEN

Quinn loves flowers and has persuaded the rest of the dragons to join her on a visit to a tulip garden. She can't wait to study all the different varieties and get some inspiration for a new horn accessory.

Stella hasn't wasted any time and has found a colourful flowerbed to explore, while Frost has been distracted by some birds. Draco isn't convinced that flowers are his thing, so he's skulked off by himself.

Can you spot all of the dragons?

CLOCKWORK CITY

The dragons have travelled to a clockwork land renowned for its machines and steam-powered engineering. They are amazed by all the mechanical inventions that help people and animals to fly and vow not to take their natural flying abilities for granted again.

Frost has flown to the rooftops to make sure he has the best vantage point, while Violet has made friends with the locals and is about to try some authentic steam-cooked food.

Can you spot all of the dragons?

STREET MARKET

Blaze wants to do some shopping for holiday souvenirs to take home to Thunder Valley. There's so much to choose from in this market, he doesn't know where to start.

Frost is intrigued by the music these humans listen to and wants to buy some old records. Moonbeam is on the hunt for some decent food. It's been a while since she's eaten her favourite snack, dragonfly skewers, but a burger will have to do for now.

Can you spot all of the dragons?

MASQUERADE BALL

The dragons love extravagant parties, so when they heard the music and spotted the sparkling lights, they couldn't resist joining in. These castle grounds are filled with glamorous guests, showing off their magical outfits and impressive dance skills.

Stella is heading for the dance floor to try out a new routine she's been practising. Blaze is just returning from a boat tour of the grounds and can't wait to join his fiery friends for a party.

Can you spot all of the dragons?

CAMBODIAN JUNGLE

The next stop on the dragons' tour is a trip into the heart of the Cambodian jungle. Quinn is excited to explore these beautiful ruins, but she's not sure where to start. She's decided to tag along with some humans who have a guidebook.

Stella's enjoying hanging out with the wildlife, but the mischievous monkeys are starting to get on Draco's nerves.

Can you spot all of the dragons?

CRYSTAL CAVES

Ever since the dragons started planning their
big trip, Violet has been looking forward to
visiting the Crystal Caves. She can't wait to
examine the gemstones and show off her
special powers – turning plain rocks into
precious stones.

Blaze is going to befriend one of the
snoozing dragons. The rest of the group
is mesmerized by the glowing treasures.
Stella has made herself at home
in a large pile of gold coins.

Can you spot all of the dragons?

FASHION SHOW

The dragons have got themselves all-access tickets to one of the hottest fashion shows of the season. Blaze is rather starstruck by all the celebrities and is trying to get himself into some paparazzi shots.

Quinn is making the most of her VIP badge and has made her way backstage. Moonbeam has no interest in waiting in the wings and is strutting her stuff on the catwalk.

Can you spot all of the dragons?

MIDNIGHT FOREST

Draco has convinced the dragons to attend a midnight dance in an enchanted forest. The full moon has attracted lots of unusual guests – from witches and wolves to ghostly beings and pixies.

Blaze is a bit shy and is checking things out from a distance before heading into the middle of the party. Frost and Moonbeam haven't wasted any time and have already made friends with a group of wood elves.

Can you spot all of the dragons?

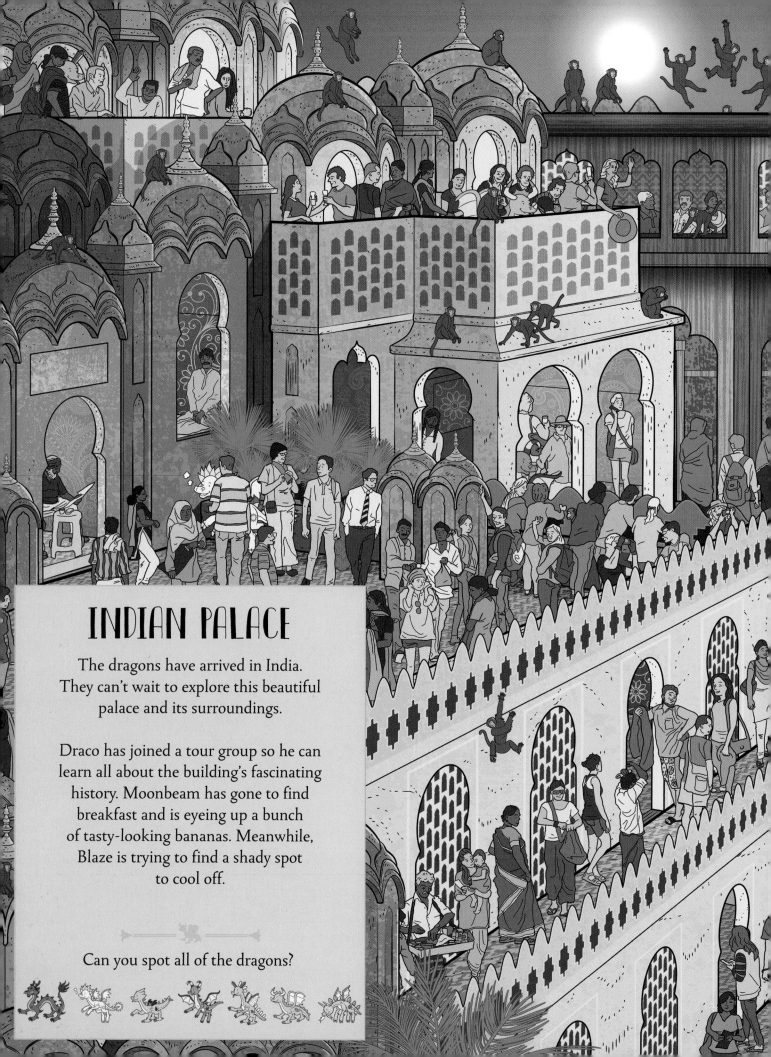

INDIAN PALACE

The dragons have arrived in India. They can't wait to explore this beautiful palace and its surroundings.

Draco has joined a tour group so he can learn all about the building's fascinating history. Moonbeam has gone to find breakfast and is eyeing up a bunch of tasty-looking bananas. Meanwhile, Blaze is trying to find a shady spot to cool off.

Can you spot all of the dragons?

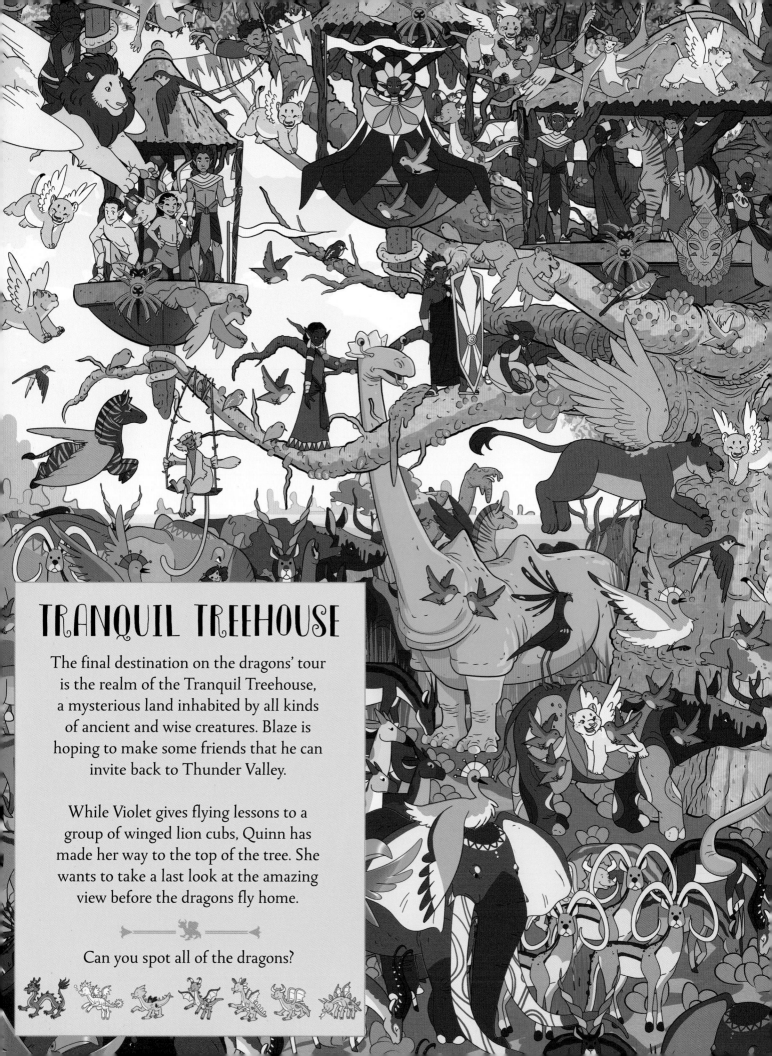

TRANQUIL TREEHOUSE

The final destination on the dragons' tour is the realm of the Tranquil Treehouse, a mysterious land inhabited by all kinds of ancient and wise creatures. Blaze is hoping to make some friends that he can invite back to Thunder Valley.

While Violet gives flying lessons to a group of winged lion cubs, Quinn has made her way to the top of the tree. She wants to take a last look at the amazing view before the dragons fly home.

Can you spot all of the dragons?

ANSWERS

SPOTTER'S CHECKLIST

A snake in a vase ☐

A woman petting a fox ☐

A golden monkey ☐

Someone feeding two dragons ☐

A man reading a scroll to a bird ☐

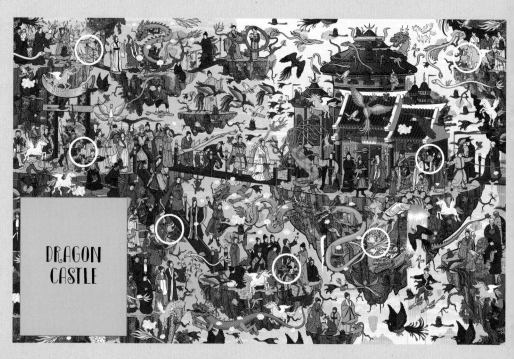

DRAGON CASTLE

DAY OF THE DEAD

SPOTTER'S CHECKLIST

A yellow parasol ☐

A man taking a photo ☐

A boy letting go of his balloon ☐

A small brown dog ☐

A child having their face painted ☐

MAGICAL MAZE

SPOTTER'S CHECKLIST

A green witch ☐

A knight with a lance ☐

An Egyptian mummy ☐

A red-haired centaur ☐

A walking, talking tree ☐

SPOTTER'S CHECKLIST

A girl with a flower on her backpack ☐

Two plain, white hot-air balloons ☐

A big bunch of ordinary balloons ☐

A sun-shaped hot-air balloon ☐

A boy in a tent ☐

BALLOON FESTIVAL

ROCKY WILDERNESS

SPOTTER'S CHECKLIST

Thirteen magical birds ☐

An airship ☐

A green rock dragon ☐

A sleeping horse with a blue coat and a purple mane and tail ☐

A yellow horse playing with a grey stone ball ☐

FAIRGROUND FUN

FLIGHT SCHOOL

TULIP GARDEN

CLOCKWORK CITY

SPOTTER'S CHECKLIST

Two clockwork peacocks ☐

A robot being wound up ☐

A clockwork snake ☐

A twin girl with a pink fan ☐

A woman wearing green boots ☐

SPOTTER'S CHECKLIST

A woman spilling her drink ☐

A golden teapot ☐

A broken record ☐

A man sitting on the floor ☐

A bowl of fish ☐

STREET MARKET

MASQUERADE BALL

SPOTTER'S CHECKLIST

A glass slipper being returned ☐

Three fauns playing pipes ☐

Six grey rabbits ☐

Two blue and yellow headdresses ☐

Someone dropping a tray of cupcakes ☐

CAMBODIAN JUNGLE

CRYSTAL CAVES

FASHION SHOW

MIDNIGHT
FOREST

SPOTTER'S CHECKLIST

Two cauldrons ☐

A wolf pup pulling on a dress hem ☐

Two witches wearing black hats ☐

An owl family ☐

A spider in a web ☐

SPOTTER'S CHECKLIST

A man meditating ☐

Three camels ☐

A man with a monkey on his shoulder ☐

A woman with an umbrella ☐

Three snakes ☐

INDIAN
PALACE

TRANQUIL
TREEHOUSE

SPOTTER'S CHECKLIST

Two elves picking pink fruit ☐

Three rhinos with trees for horns ☐

A row of three birds on a branch ☐

An elf with a large shield ☐

A purple elephant with blue ears ☐

First published in Great Britain in 2021 by Michael O'Mara Books Limited,
9 Lion Yard, Tremadoc Road, London SW4 7NQ

W www.mombooks.com   f Michael O'Mara Books   🐦 @OMaraBooks   📷 @omarabooks

Material in this book previously appeared in *Where's the Unicorn in Wonderland?* and *Where's the Llama?*

A CIP catalogue record for this book is available from the British Library.

ISBN: 978-1-78929-307-4

1 3 5 7 9 10 8 6 4 2

This book was printed in July 2021 by Shenzhen Wing King
Tong Paper Products Co. Ltd., Shenzhen, Guangdong, China.